EMMANUEL JOSEPH

The Connected Leader, How Public Speaking, Action, and Emotional Intelligence Redefine Leadership

Copyright © 2025 by Emmanuel Joseph

All rights reserved. No part of this publication may be reproduced, stored or transmitted in any form or by any means, electronic, mechanical, photocopying, recording, scanning, or otherwise without written permission from the publisher. It is illegal to copy this book, post it to a website, or distribute it by any other means without permission.

First edition

This book was professionally typeset on Reedsy.
Find out more at reedsy.com

Contents

1	Chapter 1: The New Era of Leadership	1
2	Chapter 2: The Power of Public Speaking	2
3	Chapter 3: Mastering the Art of Persuasion	3
4	Chapter 4: Action-Oriented Leadership	5
5	Chapter 5: The Role of Emotional Intelligence	6
6	Chapter 6: Building Trust through Transparency	7
7	Chapter 7: Effective Communication Strategies	8
8	Chapter 8: Leading with Empathy	9
9	Chapter 9: Inspiring Innovation and Creativity	10
10	Chapter 10: The Impact of Body Language	11
11	Chapter 11: Navigating Change and Uncertainty	12
12	Chapter 12: Building a Collaborative Culture	13
13	Chapter 13: Leading Remote and Diverse Teams	14
14	Chapter 14: The Role of Technology in Leadership	15
15	Chapter 15: Developing Future Leaders	17
16	Chapter 16: Measuring Leadership Success	18
17	Chapter 17: The Legacy of a Connected Leader	19

1

Chapter 1: The New Era of Leadership

In the dynamic and fast-paced world we live in, leadership is undergoing a profound transformation. The traditional models of authority and control are being replaced by a new paradigm—one that emphasizes connection, empathy, and communication. This chapter introduces the concept of the connected leader, who leverages public speaking, decisive action, and emotional intelligence to inspire and guide their teams.

Leadership today is not just about directing others; it is about connecting with them on a deeper level. The connected leader understands that to lead effectively, they must first build strong relationships with their team members. This involves listening, understanding, and responding to the needs and concerns of others. By doing so, they create an environment of trust and collaboration, where everyone feels valued and empowered to contribute their best.

Public speaking is a critical skill for the connected leader. It is through their words and presence that leaders can articulate their vision, share their passion, and rally others to their cause. Effective public speaking goes beyond mere rhetoric; it involves connecting with the audience on an emotional level, conveying authenticity, and inspiring action. In this chapter, we will explore how public speaking can be a powerful tool for leadership and how to harness its potential to create lasting impact.

2

Chapter 2: The Power of Public Speaking

Public speaking has always been an essential component of effective leadership, but in the context of the connected leader, it takes on even greater significance. The ability to communicate clearly, persuasively, and empathetically is crucial for building trust and fostering a sense of community. In this chapter, we delve into the nuances of public speaking and how it can be used to enhance leadership effectiveness.

At its core, public speaking is about sharing a message with an audience. However, for the connected leader, it is also about creating a connection with the audience. This involves understanding the audience's needs, tailoring the message to resonate with them, and delivering it in a way that is engaging and inspiring. Whether addressing a small team or a large crowd, the connected leader uses public speaking as a means to bridge gaps, build relationships, and drive positive change.

One of the key aspects of public speaking for connected leaders is authenticity. Authentic leaders are those who speak from the heart, who are true to themselves, and who are transparent in their communication. By being authentic, leaders build trust with their audience, as people are more likely to follow someone they perceive as genuine and trustworthy. In this chapter, we will explore techniques for developing authentic public speaking skills and how to use them to inspire and lead effectively.

3

Chapter 3: Mastering the Art of Persuasion

Persuasion lies at the heart of effective leadership. The ability to influence others and inspire them to take action is essential for achieving organizational goals. Connected leaders understand that persuasion is not about manipulation but about presenting ideas in a compelling and ethical manner. In this chapter, we explore the principles of effective persuasion and how leaders can use it to motivate and engage their teams.

Understanding the audience is the first step in mastering the art of persuasion. Leaders must be attuned to the needs, concerns, and motivations of their team members. By empathizing with their audience, leaders can craft messages that resonate on a personal level. This involves not only addressing logical arguments but also appealing to emotions. Emotional appeals, when used appropriately, can strengthen the connection between leaders and their teams, making the message more impactful.

Authenticity and transparency are crucial in persuasive communication. People are more likely to be influenced by leaders they perceive as genuine and trustworthy. Connected leaders build trust by being honest about their intentions and consistent in their actions. By demonstrating integrity, leaders can create a foundation of trust that enhances their persuasive abilities. In this chapter, we will discuss techniques for crafting persuasive messages and the ethical considerations involved in influencing others.

4

Chapter 4: Action-Oriented Leadership

While communication is vital, it is the actions of leaders that ultimately define their effectiveness. Action-oriented leadership emphasizes the importance of making informed decisions and taking decisive steps to achieve goals. Connected leaders lead by example, showing their teams that they are committed to their vision and willing to put in the effort to make it a reality.

Decisive action requires a balance between strategic thinking and agility. Leaders must be able to analyze situations, weigh options, and make informed choices quickly. This involves taking calculated risks and being adaptable in the face of changing circumstances. In this chapter, we explore the principles of action-oriented leadership, including the importance of setting clear goals, being proactive, and maintaining focus.

Leading by example is a powerful way to inspire and motivate teams. When leaders demonstrate the behaviors and values they expect from their team members, they create a culture of accountability and excellence. By aligning their actions with their words, connected leaders build trust and credibility. We will discuss strategies for effective decision-making, risk management, and leading with integrity in this chapter.

5

Chapter 5: The Role of Emotional Intelligence

Emotional intelligence (EI) is a critical component of connected leadership. It encompasses the ability to understand and manage one's own emotions, as well as the emotions of others. Leaders with high emotional intelligence are better equipped to navigate complex interpersonal dynamics and build strong, cohesive teams.

Self-awareness is the foundation of emotional intelligence. Leaders must be attuned to their own emotions, recognizing how they impact their thoughts and behaviors. By developing self-awareness, leaders can regulate their emotions, maintain composure under pressure, and make more rational decisions. In this chapter, we explore techniques for enhancing self-awareness and self-regulation.

Empathy is another key aspect of emotional intelligence. Connected leaders understand and appreciate the perspectives of others, which allows them to build deeper connections with their team members. Empathy fosters a supportive and inclusive work environment, where individuals feel valued and understood. We will discuss practical strategies for developing empathy and leveraging it to strengthen leadership effectiveness.

6

Chapter 6: Building Trust through Transparency

Trust is the cornerstone of effective leadership, and transparency is the key to building and maintaining that trust. Connected leaders understand the importance of being open and honest with their teams. This chapter explores the role of transparency in leadership and how it fosters a culture of trust and collaboration.

Transparency in leadership involves clear and open communication. Leaders must be willing to share information about the organization's goals, challenges, and decisions. By providing context and rationale, leaders help their teams understand the bigger picture and feel more invested in their work. This openness not only builds trust but also empowers team members to contribute their ideas and take ownership of their roles.

Honesty and accountability are essential components of transparent leadership. Leaders who admit their mistakes and take responsibility for their actions set a powerful example for their teams. This creates an environment where team members feel safe to speak up, share their concerns, and learn from their experiences. In this chapter, we discuss strategies for fostering transparency, including regular updates, open-door policies, and active listening.

7

Chapter 7: Effective Communication Strategies

Communication is the lifeblood of leadership. Connected leaders excel in conveying their messages clearly and effectively, ensuring that their teams are aligned and motivated. This chapter delves into various communication strategies that enhance leadership effectiveness.

Active listening is a fundamental aspect of effective communication. Leaders must not only speak but also listen to their team members, understanding their perspectives and concerns. By practicing active listening, leaders demonstrate respect and empathy, which strengthens their relationships with their teams. This chapter explores techniques for improving active listening skills and creating a culture of open dialogue.

Clear messaging is another critical element of effective communication. Leaders must articulate their vision, goals, and expectations in a way that is easily understood by their teams. This involves avoiding jargon, using simple language, and providing specific examples. Nonverbal communication, such as body language and facial expressions, also plays a significant role in conveying messages. We will discuss how leaders can use nonverbal cues to enhance their communication and build rapport with their teams.

8

Chapter 8: Leading with Empathy

Empathy is a powerful tool for leaders. It allows them to connect with their team members on a deeper level and create a supportive work environment. In this chapter, we examine the role of empathy in leadership and how it fosters a culture of inclusion and collaboration.

Empathetic leaders understand the emotions and experiences of their team members. They take the time to listen, show compassion, and offer support. By doing so, they build strong, trusting relationships that enhance team cohesion and productivity. This chapter explores practical strategies for developing and practicing empathy, including active listening, asking open-ended questions, and providing constructive feedback.

Empathy also plays a crucial role in conflict resolution. Leaders who approach conflicts with empathy are better equipped to understand the underlying issues and address them effectively. By focusing on the needs and feelings of all parties involved, empathetic leaders can facilitate constructive conversations and find mutually beneficial solutions. We will discuss techniques for resolving conflicts with empathy and maintaining a harmonious work environment.

9

Chapter 9: Inspiring Innovation and Creativity

Innovation and creativity are essential for organizational growth and success. Connected leaders inspire their teams to think creatively and embrace new ideas. This chapter explores how leaders can foster a culture of innovation and creativity within their organizations.

Encouraging experimentation is a key aspect of fostering creativity. Leaders must create an environment where team members feel safe to take risks and try new approaches. This involves celebrating successes and learning from failures, rather than punishing mistakes. By promoting a growth mindset, leaders can inspire their teams to think outside the box and come up with innovative solutions.

Supporting diverse perspectives is another important element of fostering creativity. Leaders should actively seek out and value the unique viewpoints of their team members. This diversity of thought can lead to more creative and effective solutions. In this chapter, we discuss strategies for encouraging diverse perspectives, including promoting inclusivity, facilitating brainstorming sessions, and providing opportunities for cross-functional collaboration.

10

Chapter 10: The Impact of Body Language

Body language is a powerful form of nonverbal communication that can significantly influence how a leader's message is received. Connected leaders are aware of the signals they send through their posture, gestures, and facial expressions, and they use body language to enhance their communication. This chapter explores the importance of body language in leadership and provides tips for using it effectively.

Body language can convey confidence, openness, and authority, or it can undermine a leader's message by signaling insecurity, closed-mindedness, or indecision. Leaders must be mindful of their body language and ensure that it aligns with their verbal communication. This involves maintaining good posture, making eye contact, and using appropriate gestures to emphasize key points. In this chapter, we discuss techniques for developing positive body language habits and how to interpret the nonverbal cues of others.

Nonverbal communication also plays a crucial role in building trust and rapport with team members. Leaders who use open and approachable body language create an environment where team members feel comfortable and valued. This chapter explores how leaders can use body language to foster a sense of inclusion and connection within their teams.

11

Chapter 11: Navigating Change and Uncertainty

Change is a constant in today's world, and connected leaders must navigate it effectively. This chapter covers strategies for leading through change, including resilience, adaptability, and proactive planning. Leaders who can guide their teams through periods of uncertainty and disruption are better positioned to achieve long-term success.

Resilience is the ability to bounce back from setbacks and persevere in the face of challenges. Connected leaders cultivate resilience by maintaining a positive outlook, learning from failures, and staying focused on their goals. This chapter explores techniques for building resilience, including mindfulness practices, stress management, and maintaining a healthy work-life balance.

Adaptability is another crucial skill for navigating change. Leaders must be able to pivot and adjust their strategies in response to new information and evolving circumstances. This involves being open to new ideas, embracing innovation, and encouraging a culture of continuous learning. In this chapter, we discuss strategies for fostering adaptability within teams and organizations.

12

Chapter 12: Building a Collaborative Culture

Collaboration is key to organizational success. Connected leaders build a culture of collaboration by fostering teamwork, encouraging open dialogue, and creating an environment where everyone's contributions are valued. In this chapter, we explore the benefits of collaboration and provide strategies for building and maintaining a collaborative culture.

Effective collaboration involves clear communication, mutual respect, and a shared sense of purpose. Leaders must create opportunities for team members to work together, share ideas, and support one another. This chapter discusses techniques for promoting collaboration, including team-building activities, cross-functional projects, and regular feedback sessions.

Leaders also play a crucial role in addressing and resolving conflicts that may arise within teams. By approaching conflicts with empathy and a focus on finding common ground, leaders can help their teams navigate disagreements and maintain a positive working environment. In this chapter, we explore strategies for conflict resolution and how to create a culture of collaboration and cooperation.

13

Chapter 13: Leading Remote and Diverse Teams

The modern workplace is increasingly remote and diverse. Connected leaders must adapt to leading teams that are geographically dispersed and culturally diverse. This chapter examines the challenges and opportunities of leading remote and diverse teams, including communication, inclusion, and building a sense of belonging.

Leading remote teams requires effective use of technology and clear communication. Leaders must ensure that remote team members feel connected and engaged, despite the physical distance. This involves using video conferencing, messaging platforms, and other tools to facilitate communication and collaboration. In this chapter, we discuss strategies for leading remote teams, including setting clear expectations, providing regular updates, and fostering a sense of community.

Cultural diversity brings unique perspectives and strengths to a team, but it can also present challenges. Leaders must be aware of cultural differences and foster an inclusive environment where everyone feels valued and respected. This chapter explores techniques for promoting cultural competence, including diversity training, inclusive policies, and celebrating cultural differences.

14

Chapter 14: The Role of Technology in Leadership

Technology is transforming the way we lead, enabling greater connectivity, efficiency, and innovation. Connected leaders leverage technology to enhance their effectiveness, from communication tools to data analytics. In this chapter, we explore the impact of technology on leadership and discuss how leaders can use it to improve decision-making, streamline processes, and stay connected with their teams.

Effective use of technology starts with choosing the right tools for communication and collaboration. Leaders must stay informed about the latest technological advancements and select platforms that best meet their team's needs. This includes video conferencing, project management software, and instant messaging apps. In this chapter, we discuss the benefits and challenges of various technologies and provide tips for integrating them into the workflow.

Data-driven decision-making is another crucial aspect of leveraging technology in leadership. Connected leaders use data analytics to gain insights into team performance, identify trends, and make informed decisions. By harnessing the power of data, leaders can improve efficiency, optimize resources, and achieve better outcomes. We will explore techniques for collecting and analyzing data, as well as the ethical considerations involved in data-driven leadership.

15

Chapter 15: Developing Future Leaders

Connected leaders are committed to developing the next generation of leaders. This chapter covers strategies for mentoring, coaching, and supporting emerging leaders. By investing in leadership development, leaders ensure the long-term success and sustainability of their organizations.

Mentoring and coaching are powerful tools for developing future leaders. Leaders must provide guidance, feedback, and support to help their team members grow and reach their potential. This involves identifying individuals with leadership potential, setting clear development goals, and offering opportunities for growth. In this chapter, we discuss techniques for effective mentoring and coaching, including active listening, goal-setting, and providing constructive feedback.

Creating a culture of continuous learning is essential for leadership development. Leaders must encourage their teams to pursue ongoing education, skill development, and professional growth. This can be achieved through training programs, workshops, and access to resources. In this chapter, we explore strategies for fostering a learning culture, including promoting curiosity, supporting experimentation, and recognizing achievements.

16

Chapter 16: Measuring Leadership Success

Success in leadership is not just about achieving goals; it's also about the impact leaders have on their teams and organizations. In this chapter, we explore various metrics for measuring leadership success, including employee engagement, team performance, and organizational outcomes. By assessing their effectiveness, leaders can identify areas for improvement and celebrate their accomplishments.

Employee engagement is a key indicator of leadership success. Engaged employees are more motivated, productive, and committed to their work. Leaders must regularly assess engagement levels through surveys, feedback sessions, and one-on-one meetings. In this chapter, we discuss strategies for improving employee engagement, including fostering a positive work environment, recognizing achievements, and addressing concerns.

Team performance is another important metric for measuring leadership success. Leaders must evaluate how well their teams are meeting their goals and objectives. This involves setting clear performance indicators, monitoring progress, and providing support as needed. In this chapter, we explore techniques for assessing team performance and identifying areas for improvement.

17

Chapter 17: The Legacy of a Connected Leader

A connected leader's legacy is defined by the positive impact they have on others. This final chapter reflects on the journey of becoming a connected leader and the enduring influence of public speaking, action, and emotional intelligence. We discuss how leaders can leave a lasting legacy by inspiring others, fostering a culture of excellence, and making a meaningful difference in the world.

The legacy of a connected leader is built on the relationships they create and the lives they touch. By leading with empathy, authenticity, and integrity, leaders leave a lasting impression on their teams and organizations. This chapter explores the qualities that define a connected leader's legacy and how these qualities can inspire others to follow in their footsteps.

Fostering a culture of excellence is another important aspect of a connected leader's legacy. Leaders must set high standards for themselves and their teams, encouraging continuous improvement and innovation. By promoting a culture of excellence, leaders ensure that their organizations thrive long after they have moved on. In this chapter, we discuss strategies for creating and maintaining a culture of excellence.

Making a meaningful difference in the world is the ultimate goal of a connected leader. By using their influence to drive positive change, leaders can leave a lasting legacy that extends beyond their immediate organizations. This chapter explores how leaders can leverage their skills, knowledge, and networks to make a positive impact on their communities and the world at large.

The Connected Leader: How Public Speaking, Action, and Emotional Intelligence Redefine Leadership

In a rapidly evolving world, the traditional models of leadership no longer suffice. "The Connected Leader" delves into the transformative power of modern leadership, where public speaking, decisive action, and emotional intelligence converge to redefine what it means to lead effectively. This comprehensive guide explores how today's leaders can harness these elements to inspire and connect with their teams, foster innovation, and drive lasting change.

Discover the importance of public speaking in articulating vision and building trust, the necessity of taking informed and decisive action, and the profound impact of emotional intelligence on leadership effectiveness. Through practical strategies, real-life examples, and insightful reflections, this book provides a roadmap for aspiring and seasoned leaders alike.

Whether you are looking to enhance your communication skills, build stronger relationships with your team, or navigate the complexities of change and uncertainty, "The Connected Leader" offers valuable insights and actionable advice. Join the ranks of leaders who are not just commanding authority, but truly connecting with and uplifting those they lead.

www.ingramcontent.com/pod-product-compliance
Lightning Source LLC
LaVergne TN
LVHW010445070526
838199LV00066B/6216